HISTORY QUICK READS

BRITAIN SINCE 1948

Under the Counter

Ice-Cream Annie

The Monster Rat

by David Oakden

Illustrated by Gillian Marklew

ANGLIA BOOKS
young

First published in 2003
by Anglia Young Books

Anglia Young Books is an imprint of
Mill Publishing Ltd
PO Box 120
Bangor
County Down BT19 7BX

Illustrations by Gillian Marklew
Design by Angela Ashton

British Library Cataloguing-in-Publication Data

A catalogue record for this book is available from the British Library

ISBN 1 871173 90 6

Printed in Great Britain by Ashford Colour Press, Gosport, Hampshire

CONTENTS

UNDER THE COUNTER

'Can I stay up tonight to see in the New Year?' asked Molly. 'My friend Lizzie is going to stay up with her dad and mum and the little ones. They're all going to drink sherry and smoke cigars.'

Molly's mum sniffed. 'Oh yes? Her new baby will be drinking and smoking? I don't think so. No, Molly, you'll be up those stairs to bed, as usual, at seven o'clock. You can wait for 1949 until you get up.'

'It's not fair,' said Molly.

'Fair's fair. You're eight years old and you can go to bed late and drink and smoke when you're twenty-one, if you are daft enough. But that's enough about that. Are you going to come shopping with me? I need your help to carry the bags.'

Molly put away her box of crayons and exercise book. They had been a Christmas present from her Aunt Sophie. She put her special rubber, shaped like a rabbit, into her pocket.

'Are we going to get some sweets?' she said. 'Can I have some of that white chocolate? Lizzie says her dad's got a cupboard full of it. He got it from a man who works on the railway. He says it fell off the back of a truck and nobody wanted it.'

Molly's mum raised her eyes to the ceiling. 'Fell off the back of a truck, indeed,' she muttered. Then she went on, 'Just hurry up and put your coat on.'

'Please can we get some chocolate,' begged Molly.

'No,' said her mum. 'There will be no chocolate, because we've used our <u>ration</u> for the month. But we have got enough meat <u>coupons</u> for some stewing beef, so we'll go to the butcher's. We might be lucky. Mr Johnson might let us have some sausages or a bit of liver. They're not rationed, but he never seems to have any when I ask.'

'Lizzie's mum says he only lets his pals have it,' said Molly, fastening the belt on her school coat.

'Don't tell me any more about Lizzie or her mum. Just put on that woolly hat that your gran knitted for you and those gloves that we got off the <u>rummage sale</u> last week.'

They walked out of the house. Mum shut the front door with a bang. 'Must get your dad to see to the lock,' she said. 'Somebody said that they had burglars up the road. We shall have to start locking all the doors and windows when we go out. Before the war we never used to bother. Times have changed.'

They turned the corner into the main street. 'Look,' said Molly. 'The grocery has got raspberry jam. Pots of it. Can we have some?'

'Sorry,' said Mum. 'If we have that then we can't have any sugar this week. I used all our ration over Christmas, so no more jam, honey or sugar until next Monday when the new ration books come.'

'I'm sick of rations,' said Molly.

Soon they reached the butcher's shop. Outside there was a queue of women with shopping baskets. It was cold and windy and they had all pulled up their coat collars.

'Queues,' grumbled Mum. 'We never had queues before the war. Here we are at the end of 1948 and things are still just as bad.'

The queue moved slowly. One by one the women went in and came out with their small pieces of meat, wrapped in greaseproof paper and newspaper. One woman came out with an extra packet, and the other women started to grumble. 'See her,' said one. 'That's her from the cigarette <u>kiosk</u> down by the station. I bet she got some sausages. She lets Mr Johnson have those American cigarettes she keeps hidden.'

Everyone started to say nasty things about the butcher, but then it was Mum's turn. She handed over her ration book.

'One shilling and sevenpence left on your coupons,' said Mr Johnson. He chopped off a page from the book with a huge knife. 'You could have those four <u>mutton</u> chops or some stewing beef.'

'Beef,' said Mum. 'Chop bones weigh too much. Oh, and I'll have some of the sausages you let that lady have just now.'

'Sausages?' said Mr Johnson. 'We've got no sausages. Haven't had any for a month.'

Molly had been using her rabbit-shaped rubber to get dirty finger-marks off the posters on the wall. One poster said, "Waste not, Want not. Boil your bones for soup."

Somebody had written in pencil, "And boil your head for a football."

Molly rubbed at the words, but the rubber jumped out of her hand and fell into the sawdust on the floor. She bent down to find it, but it had bounced under the counter flap and was by Mr Johnson's feet. Molly crawled after it, and as she did so she saw a shelf under the counter. On the shelf was a tray. And the tray was heaped high with sausages.

Mum was just paying Mr Johnson. He was grumbling because she had given him a ten-shilling note and it was using up all his change.

Molly pulled Mum's coat. 'Under the counter,' she said. 'Sausages. Hundreds of them. All fat and juicy.'

Mum took her change and then put her mouth very close to Mr Johnson's ear. Molly couldn't hear what she said, but Mr Johnson scowled and the next minute Mum handed over more money and a little parcel changed hands.

Mr Johnson whispered, 'Don't tell anybody.'

When they got out of the shop and were walking up the street, Mum suddenly stopped and hugged Molly. 'Clever girl,' she said. 'We've got eight beautiful sausages. I just told him that I knew what he had got under the counter, and if he didn't let me buy some I should tell all the other women.'

'So you didn't tell them,' said Molly.

Mum grinned. 'I didn't need to. I just told old Granny Potts at the back of the queue. She will soon tell the rest what you saw under that counter. Serve that butcher right. Perhaps he'll be fair to all his customers now and stop giving the off-ration bits to his favourites.'

Molly said, 'I got you the sausages, Mum. So can we have some raspberry jam?'

'No. Sorry. Anyway, your grandad says it's not made from raspberries. He says it's just mashed-up turnips, coloured red. And the seeds aren't real. They are made of wood.'

Molly sighed. 'Our teacher said that when the war ended everybody thought that there would be plenty of food.'

'That's right,' said Mum. 'That's what we all thought.'

Molly smiled to herself. But tonight they would have a treat. They would have sausages. And perhaps Mum would let her stay up to see in the New Year after all.

Historical Notes
for Under the Counter (1948)

Christmas presents in 1948 were few and cheap. Children would be pleased to get a small gift like a new book to read or an exercise book to write and draw in. That would be all, except for a few sweets in their stockings along with an apple, an orange and a cracker. Molly's rubber would have been a very special treat. Lizzie's dad, who had chocolate that fell off the back of a lorry, could have been sent to prison for taking part in stealing rationed food.

Butchers had a hard job, even though the war was over. Meat was still rationed so that families had only a very little meat to eat. Some meats, such as sausages, liver, brains and bones, were off the ration. Butchers had to let customers have these fairly, but often their special friends got more than the others. Fights in meat queues were not unknown if the news got out that somebody had had special treatment.

Grandad's story about raspberry jam was a common one; wartime rationing and shortages made families eat all kinds of odd things. But whether it was a true story or not nobody seems to know!

Glossary

- ration – the amount of food each person was allowed to buy per week.

- coupons – books of tickets which people had to hand in when buying their rations.

- rummage sale – jumble sale.

- grocery – a shop selling goods such as tea, sugar, butter, flour, tinned food, etc.

- kiosk – booth.

- mutton – meat from older sheep.

- ten-shilling note – old bank note, worth fifty pence in today's money.

ICE-CREAM ANNIE

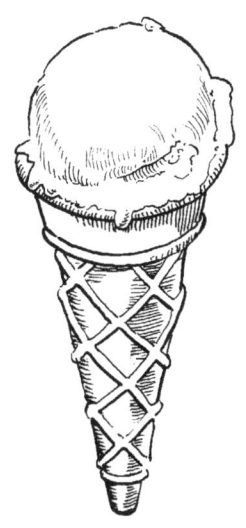

It was a sunny day in 1955. At school there was
a new girl in Annie's class. She had dark hair
and the teacher sent her to sit by Annie. 'We've
just moved,' said the new girl. 'We got one of
those new council houses that were built last
year for <u>coal-miners</u>. My dad's a miner, but the
pit up North ran out of coal and there's plenty
down here.'

The teacher heard her. 'That's right, Susan,' she
said. 'There's plenty of coal here. Enough
to drive our two new power stations.'

'Do you want to come out with me on Saturday morning, Susan?' whispered Annie. 'I'm going to the <u>pictures</u>. It's <u>Tarzan</u> and they say it's smashing. Why don't you come too?'

'I'd like to,' said Susan, 'but I haven't got any money. Dad hasn't had his first wages yet.'

'It's only <u>fourpence</u>,' said Annie. 'Oh, and another <u>twopence</u> for an ice-cream.'

'I can do without ice-cream,' said Susan.

Annie said, 'But that's the best part. I love ice-cream.'

'So do I,' said Susan. 'I'll try to come.'

On Saturday morning, Annie got her <u>sixpence</u>, her week's pocket money. Her mum had also given her threepence on Friday for helping weed the front garden, but she had spent that on one of the new <u>biros</u> from Woolworth's.

'Hm,' said Grandma. 'In my day we had a pot of ink in a little hole in the desk and wooden pens with steel nibs. These ball-point things look good.'

When Annie and Susan met later that morning, Annie said, 'Have you got your sixpence?'

'Only twopence,' said Susan. 'Sorry. That means I can't go.'

Annie grinned. 'No. We've got enough between us. Six and two make eight and that's two fours,' she said. 'We can do without ices.'

There were about a hundred children in the queue for the pictures. The manager, Mr Victor, stood on the steps. 'You!' he shouted at a boy. 'You're chewing gum. Spit it out. Anybody else got any?'

Everybody pretended to chew. A hundred jaws moved up and down and voices said, 'Gee, man,

this gum sure is the tops.' And, 'Howdy partner. This sure is sticky stuff.'

Mr Victor gave up. He opened the doors and the children rushed in.

'Not in the front row,' said Annie. 'Grab those two near the end, then we shall be near Mrs Victor when she comes round with the ices.'

'Not much point in that,' said Susan. 'We have no money, remember.'

'Well, sit there anyway.'

The lights went down and the screen showed advertisements. The one for Walls Choc-Ices made Annie lick her lips. Next came a short film about Africa. The boys all jumped up and down like monkeys, then staggered into the gangways, scratching under their arm-pits.

After that came another film, specially made for children. It was dull and boring, about a girl and her brother, in very clean clothes, who trapped a gang of robbers. A policeman rode up on his bike and the robbers just walked off quietly to prison.

Nobody liked that. There was a lot of whistling, and shouts of 'Rubbish!' and 'Up the robbers!'.

Then there was a Tom and Jerry cartoon. Everybody cheered, especially when Tom the cat was thrown out of the house while Jerry the mouse ate the cat's supper.

After that it was the <u>interval</u> and the lights came on. A lot of boys and girls went to the toilets. Others just fooled about and made rude noises. Two boys and two girls went on the stage and pretended to be singers, until Mr Victor fetched them off.

Mrs Victor came with her ice-cream tray. There were choc-ices, tubs, paper-wrapped wafers and lollipops. A big boy asked for two lollipops. He gave Mrs Victor <u>half-a-crown</u> and she had to find change. She was struggling to reach into the tin box where she kept the money and at the same time stop the tray tipping over.

'Look,' said Annie. 'Look at the strap on the tray. It's breaking!'

She jumped to her feet. 'Look at your strap!' she yelled to Mrs Victor. She got up just as a boy ran past, chased by another. They both ran into Annie. She fell on her back at Mrs Victor's feet. At that moment the strap broke and everything slid off the tray.

Choc-ices and tubs fell on top of Annie. Two lollipops landed on her face and another one slid down the neck of her shirt. Then something heavy landed on her tummy. She grabbed it with both hands. It was the money-box with all the money in it.

Mr Victor came running up. 'That girl is stealing all the money,' he said. He grabbed Annie and pulled her to her feet.

'No,' said Mrs Victor. 'You've got it wrong, dear. This clever girl saw the strap breaking and tried to catch everything. She *saved* our money.'

Mr Victor's face went very red. 'Oh, sorry,' he said. 'Here, little girl, have a choc-ice. Have two. Have two tubs as well. And take some lollipops. Here, let me give you sixpence ...'

Annie didn't take the money but she did take two choc-ices. She and Susan ate them as the big film began. It was about Tarzan and the apes and it was great. 'Those apes behaved better than the boys!' said Annie.

At the end of the film everybody made a dash for the door, trying to get out before they had to stand still for the National Anthem.

Mr Victor was by the door. He gave Annie a piece of cardboard. 'It's a pass for you and your friend to get in free to any Saturday show for the rest of this year. We owe you a lot. If that money-box had come open with all those children around I don't know what would have happened.'

'Gosh,' Annie said. 'Thank you very much.'

'Wait,' said Mr Victor. 'And here's your entrance money back, too.' He handed them fourpence each.

Susan said, 'Going to the pictures with you is a real adventure! What shall we do with our fourpences?'

But Annie was already on her way into Woolworth's next door and heading for the ice-cream counter.

Historical Notes
for Ice-Cream Annie (1955)

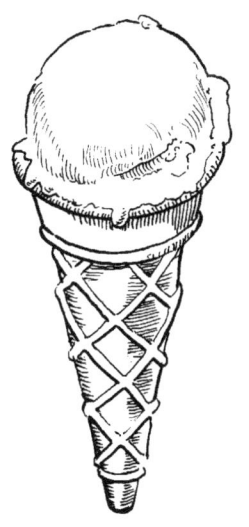

This was a time when television was very new.
Most families could not afford to have one, as
the cheapest sets, with tiny 9-inch screens, cost
£40 or £50, plus extra for an aerial, and this
was about a month's wages in 1955. So the
'pictures' (the cinema) were still very popular
and cheap, especially the Saturday morning
shows for children which had a cartoon, news
film, children's films and travel or nature films.
The show lasted about three hours and kept
children occupied for the whole morning.

Plain ice-creams and lollies (just frozen coloured ice) were very cheap, though most ice-cream was still sold by the scoop into biscuit cornets and wafers. Choc-ices were more expensive and not so common.

Susan's father had to move house to keep his job as a coal-miner. About this time, some of the old pits were running out of coal; others were so difficult to work that men had to crawl on their knees through water to get to the coal-face. The discovery of new and rich coal-seams meant the arrival in towns of hundreds of families from distant areas.

Glossary
- coal-miners – workers who dug coal from deep pits.

- pictures – the cinema.

- Tarzan – strong, clever man in books and films, who lived like a savage in the African jungle.

- fourpence/twopence/sixpence – old money. Two and a half pennies were worth one penny in today's money.

- biro – ball-point pen, invented by Mr Biro.

- interval – a short break between films at a cinema.

- half-a-crown – old coin, worth about twelve pence today.

- National Anthem – 'God Save the Queen', which was played at the end of every film show.

THE MONSTER RAT

Mr Berry was at the top of a stepladder, hanging wallpaper. The wallpaper was covered with flowers.

'Dad,' said George. 'My electric train's bust.'

'Don't bother me now, George,' said Mr Berry. 'Can't you see I'm busy? And turn that record player off. I'm tired of the Beatles.' He climbed down the stepladder and looked at the wallpaper.

'That will have to do,' he said.

'But Dad,' said George, 'the school's been given a model of *The Rocket* – the first <u>steam locomotive</u> – and we're having a special display. I promised I would take my train.'

'Steam trains were great,' said his father, as he wiped his hands on his dungarees. 'Better than these silly little <u>diesels</u> and better-looking than the electric trains. All those wires spoil the look of the stations.'

'*Please* mend the train, Dad,' said George.

'I'm always mending things for you, George. I've only just finished mending the school hamster's cage.'

'It wasn't very well mended,' muttered George. 'Hammy got out again yesterday. We looked for him all over the school, but we couldn't find him.'

Mr Berry didn't hear. He was too busy frowning at the wallpaper.

'The wallpaper looks really good, Dad,' said George, more loudly. 'And if you mend the train I won't tell Mum that you've hung that piece upside-down!'

It was time for school. George climbed over the garden fence and called for his pal, Charlie. Charlie came out of the back door. His mouth was full of <u>Sugar Frosties</u>.

'Guess what,' he said. 'My big brother's got a car. This year's <u>Ford Capri</u>. 1965 model with <u>bench seats</u>, radio, heater and a twin-tone hooter. He reckons you could cram five in the front and six in the back – that's all the soccer team.'

George said, 'My Dad thinks seat-belts will soon be here. Then everybody will have to be belted in.'

'Seat-belts!' said Charlie. 'That's a funny idea.'

They walked up the road together. The school was new. It had two storeys, a flat roof, and a large playing field. There was even a bike rack for the teachers' bikes. Inside, the hall was fitted out with PE equipment and there was a kitchen gleaming with stainless steel. Everybody liked the school. It was so much better than the old building with its outside toilets and leaky roof.

The day went well. Mrs Lewis, their teacher, showed them the splendid model steam locomotive, *The Rocket*. Then they all worked on the display. George and Charlie made and painted a huge poster of a railway station and a station-master with a long beard and a whistle in his mouth. Behind him there was a slot machine with a label saying, "Fry's Chocolate Bars. One Penny."

School dinner was sausage, beans and chips, followed by jam pudding with custard. George called it "Cowboy's Dinner with Stodge to follow", but he ate every bit.

In the afternoon they worked on their projects. Charlie was doing one on cars and he drew his brother's new Capri. The library van arrived and George got first go at the new book called *The Borrowers*, about tiny people who lived under the floorboards. At the end of the day Mrs Lewis read a bit more of their class story, *The Hobbit*.

At going-home time, there was still no sign of Hammy the hamster.

'He'll have to stay out until Monday,' said Mrs Lewis. 'We'll leave his cage door open in case he wants to go back.'

Next morning, Saturday, there was a football match and George and Charlie were in the team. They went in the old school bus which the Head, Mr Hall, drove. Things did not go well. George missed an open goal and Charlie, who was in goal, let the ball in while he was bending down to do up his shoe-lace. The result was a 2 – 2 draw.

'Terrible,' grumbled Mr Hall. 'You played like five-year olds.' Then he pointed at George and Charlie. 'You two boys, wait behind and help me to unload the kit off the bus.'

In school everything was very quiet. While Charlie and Mr Hall put the flags and balls back in the hall cupboard, George wandered off up the corridor. Suddenly he heard a noise. It was coming from the staff-room. 'Help! Please help me!'

George shouted for Mr Hall and he came running. 'Who's in there?' he said.

'Help me!'

Mr Hall slowly opened the door. He told the boys to wait outside, but they peeped in. A man was lying on the floor. One of his legs was bent

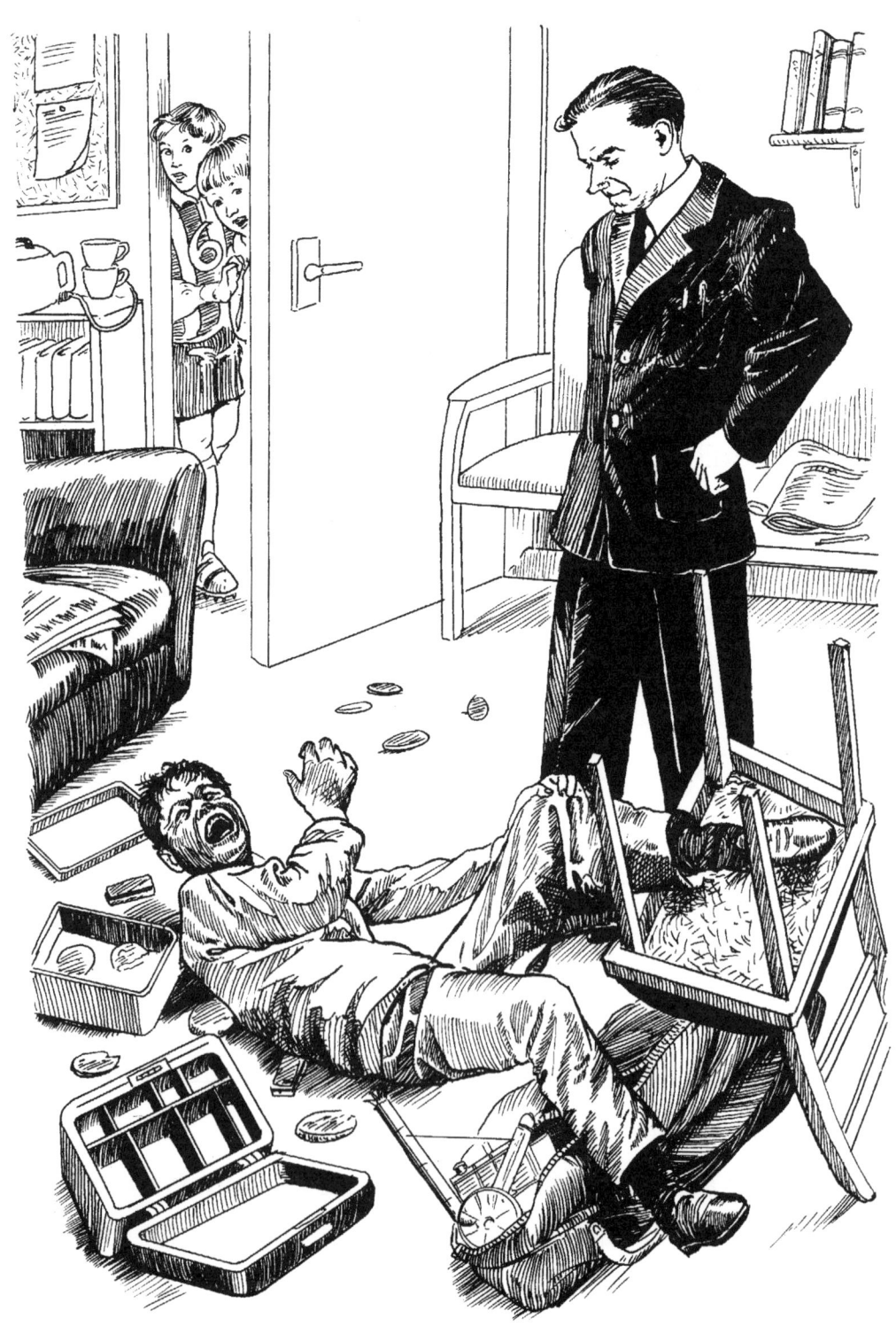

in a funny shape and one of his hands was covered in blood. There was a large bump on his head.

'Thank goodness you've come,' the man said. 'A rat jumped out of a box and bit me. Then I fell off a chair and I think my leg is broken.'

Mr Hall looked very cross and he questioned the man for a long time before he went and telephoned for an ambulance and the police. 'It's a break-in at the school,' he said. 'And we've got the burglar.'

The news was all round the town on Sunday. Everybody was saying that a large gang of cut-throat robbers had smashed all the school windows, stolen thousands of pounds and been driven out by a swarm of monster rats.

In Assembly on Monday morning Mr Hall told them what had really happened. 'The burglar got in by a window that was not locked,' he said. 'He took the model of *The Rocket* and put it in his bag. He also made a real mess of the staff-room looking for money but all he found was one <u>shilling</u> and <u>elevenpence</u>, from the teachers' tea money. Then he went to help himself to biscuits …'

'Lucky old teachers,' George whispered to Charlie. 'Why don't *we* get biscuits?'

'… and the burglar says that a monster rat leaped out of the biscuit tin and bit him. Now please tell your parents that there are no rats in this school. No rats. Please, teachers, stop those infants crying. Tell them that there are no rats in this school!'

As they went out, George had an idea. He knocked on the staff-room door. Miss Jones, the secretary, was making tea. 'Miss,' said George, 'that rat. I think I know where it is.'

'There is no rat,' said Miss Jones, firmly. 'You heard what the Headmaster said.'

But George took no notice. He went to the biscuit tin and lifted the lid.

Inside the tin was Hammy the hamster. His cheeks were bulging with biscuits and he had made a nest with old wrapping papers.

'Well, would you believe it!' said everybody when they heard. Hammy was a hero. He had bitten the burglar and made him fall off the chair and break his leg. The model of *The Rocket* was safe.

George's father mended Hammy's cage again and George made a label for it. It said, "This is Hammy the Brave. He stopped the Great Train Robbery of 1965."

Everybody liked that label, especially Hammy. He pulled it into his cage, chewed it up and made a nest of it. Then he used his teeth to undo the wire that George's father had put on the door, and went to see if he could find any more biscuits. Life was good for a hero hamster.

Historical Notes
for The Monster Rat (1965)

By 1965, twenty years after the end of the war, Britain was enjoying a prosperous age, known as the Swinging Sixties. This was the age of pop groups, rock and roll, mini-skirts and flared trousers. Groups like The Beatles and The Rolling Stones sold millions of records.

Television had become common, so that most households had one, and there was more than one station; Independent Television had arrived to rival the BBC. Cars were cheap and so was petrol, so roads began to get crowded and motorways were built. More people went on foreign holidays.

In schools, class sizes had shrunk, from more than 50 to less than 40 pupils. There was more special equipment, too, such as classroom televisions and tape recorders and lots of new books. New school buildings were bigger, brighter and surrounded by playing fields. Many schools had a minibus, bought and maintained by Parent-Teacher Associations.

Pets were common in classrooms. There were rabbits, tanks of tropical fish, mice and stick-insects. Hamsters and gerbils became popular and were kept both at home and at school.

Unfortunately, the period also saw an increase in crime. In 1963, robbers got away with over £1,000,000 in what became known as The Great Train Robbery. However, most of the gang were jailed by the following year. Schools often had break-ins, with small-time crooks stealing equipment and cash. Life was not all good in the Swinging Sixties.

Glossary

- steam locomotive – engine that used coal to make steam to drive a train.

- diesel – engine that used diesel oil to drive a train.

- Sugar Frosties – a breakfast cereal.

- Ford Capri – a car with a long body.

- bench seats – car seats that were like padded benches, stretching right across the car.

- station-master – important man in charge of a railway station.

- shilling – old coin, worth five pence in today's money.

- elevenpence – just less than a shilling. There were twelve pence in a shilling.